Photography
YEARBOOK
1989

Photography YEARBOOK 1989

Edited by

Peter Wilkinson FRPS

Fountain Press

Fountain Press Limited
45 The Broadway
Tolworth
Surrey KT6 7DW
England

ISBN 0 86343 170 4

Design and Layout by Grant Bradford

Typeset by Crowborough Typesetters

Printed and Bound by Amadeus, Italy

CONTENTS

INTRODUCTION

As has been the case for many years, so many good pictures were submitted for this edition of PHOTOGRAPHY YEARBOOK that lack of space unfortunately prevented many from being included. When making my selection, I only look at the pictures and not at their authors' names. It can sometimes happen, therefore, that when the book is finished one photographer has had a number of pictures selected, which I am certain must be rather frustrating to those who also submitted but did not have any work accepted. The content and layout must be the Editor's first priority, however, even if that occasionally means the temporary loss of a friend or two!

My association with The Royal Photographic Society, The London Salon of Photography, and the photographic trade, involves my attending most of the major overseas trade exhibitions which, fortunately, and unlike similar events in the UK, nearly always have a cultural section showing photographs. As a result, I enjoy seeing many thousands of photographs during the course of a year. But I consider my greatest photographic enjoyment of any year to be the first viewing of the material submitted for PHOTOGRAPHY YEARBOOK. These photographs originate in many countries around the world. Since the authors are from all walks of life and have widely differing interests, many of their pictures – perhaps because of unusual subject matter or camera technique – are often both original and exciting.

Two remarks are frequently overheard when a non-photographer is admiring a picture: 'You must have a good camera', and 'What camera do you use?' Yet I am certain that the same person, confronted with a painting, would not enquire as to the price or the make of the paint and canvas used by the artist. The final pages of each issue of PHOTOGRAPHY YEARBOOK are devoted to Technical Data, the bare specifics that contributed to the making of the pictures. Yet one wonders whether that list of the types and makes of cameras used might, to some extent, perpetuate the myth that an expensive camera is necessary to produce good photographs. The fact that many of the pictures submitted were taken by photographic enthusiasts, amateur and professional, means that they are very likely to have used top-of-the-range equipment, but in fact the majority of photographs could have been taken with quite simple cameras, and the results would have been virtually indistinguishable. There are, of course, exceptions; for example when very short or very long focal-length lenses are used to create an unusual perspective. During the past year Mr H.S. Fry, a regular contributor to PHOTOGRAPHY YEARBOOK, has been using a compact camera of the type that most people buy to take on holidays and for family snapshots, instead of his extensive range of expensive cameras and lenses. His results from this camera were so impressive that Nikon arranged a one-man exhibition, 'One Year with a Compact Camera', at their prestigious gallery in London. The moral of this is that it is the ability and the eye of the person using the camera that captures the picture, not just the camera. I suspect that the majority of people seeing this book – those, that is, who are not already contributors – possess cameras which, used imaginatively, could produce pictures of the standard published. Why not make that extra effort? It may well be that your work could be published in the next edition – but don't forget to submit it before the 31st January!

PHOTOGRAPHY YEARBOOK's publishers, despite the fact that the originals consist of large and small colour transparencies and prints of varying sizes in both monochrome and colour, go to great lengths to ensure that the pictures will be reproduced to the highest standards practicable. I consider, in fact, that in some instances the reproduction is an improvement on the originals! Since the publishers go to such trouble to obtain the best quality of reproduction, we appeal to contributors to help by ensuring that their prints are correctly spotted, that their slides are free from scratches and blemishes, and that their work is adequately packed before it is despatched. It is most frustrating not to be able to use a good transparency because it has a scratch, or a print because it is creased.

As the Editor of PHOTOGRAPHY YEARBOOK, I would like to join the publishers in congratulating all the contributors, and to thank all the photographers who submitted material for this edition. As always, the continuing future of the book depends on its contributors; so if you have work (or know of other photographers who have work) which you consider may be suitable for inclusion in the next edition, please let us have it before the end of January 1989. Material from overseas is always especially welcome, not least because it helps to maintain the book's international character.

Colour transparencies can be of any size, but should not be mounted in glass. Prints, both monochrome and colour, should not be smaller than 18 × 24cm, and preferably not larger than 30 × 40cm. All work should carry the author's name. Information as to the picture's location or the subject's name, any fact/s of special interest, and the make of the camera, focal length of the lens, the filter and make of film used should be included. If the packing is suitable, and postage money or International Reply Coupons are included, work will be returned after the selection, although Fountain Press Limited cannot be held responsible for any loss or damage to transparencies or prints.

As well as enjoying the prestige of having their work accepted, successful contributors will each receive a copy of PHOTOGRAPHY YEARBOOK and a reproduction fee. The copyright of any published picture remains with the author.

We look forward to seeing some of your pictures by the end of January 1989.

Peter Wilkinson, FRPS

Auch für diese Ausgabe des PHOTOGRAPHY YEARBOOK wurden, wie bereits in den vergangenen Jahren, so viele gute Aufnahmen eingeschickt, daß aus Platzgründen viele leider nicht aufgenommen werden konnten.

Bei der Auswahl schaue ich mir nur die Aufnahmen an, und nicht den Namen des Fotografen. So kann es manchmal passieren, daß, wenn das Buch fertig ist, von einem Fotografen mehrere Aufnahmen ausgewählt wurden; sicherlich ist dies frustrierend für diejenigen, deren eingeschickte Arbeiten nicht akzeptiert wurden. Für den Herausgeber müssen Inhalt und Layout jedoch den Vorrang haben, selbst wenn dies gelegentlich den zeitweisen Verlust eines oder zweier Freunde zur Folge hat!

Auf Grund meiner Zusammenarbeit mit 'The Royal Photographic Society', 'The London Salon of Photography' und dem Fotohandel besuche ich fast alle wichtigen Messen im Ausland, an die glücklicherweise (im Unterschied zu ähnlichen Ereignissen in Großbritannien) fast immer ein kultureller Teil mit einer Fotoausstellung angeschlossen ist. Auf diese Weise habe ich Gelegenheit, im Laufe eines Jahres Tausende von Fotografien zu sehen. Das größte Vergnügen auf fotografischem Gebiet jedoch bereitet mir jedes Jahr der Augenblick, in dem ich das für das PHOTOGRAPHY YEARBOOK eingeschickte Material zum ersten Mal sehe. Diese Fotografien stammen aus der ganzen Welt. Da die Fotografen aus vielen verschiedenen Lebensbereichen kommen und ganz unterschiedliche Interessen haben, sind viele ihrer Aufnahmen – auf Grund eines ungewöhnlichen Motivs etwa, oder auf Grund der Kameratechnik – originell und spannend zugleich.

Wenn ein Laie eine Fotografie bewundert, hört man oft die beiden folgenden Bemerkungen: 'Sie müssen einen guten Fotoapparat haben', und 'Welche Kamera benutzen Sie?' Ich bin jedoch sicher, daß die gleiche Person, wenn sie ein Gemälde betrachtet, weder nach dem Preis fragen würde, noch nach dem Hersteller der Farbe oder der Leinwand, die der Künstler benutzt hat. Auf den letzten Seiten in jeder Ausgabe des PHOTOGRAPHY YEARBOOK werden die technischen Daten gegeben, die bloßen näheren Einzelheiten, die zum Entstehen der Aufnahmen beigetragen haben. Hier stellt sich die Frage, ob diese Liste von Typ und Fabrikat der benutzten Fotoapparate nicht etwa, zumindest zu einem gewissen Grad, den Mythos erhärtet, daß man eine teure Kamera braucht, um gute Fotos zu machen. Da viele der eingeschickten Aufnahmen von begeisterten Fotografen, sowohl Hobby- als auch Berufsfotografen, stammen, ist anzunehmen, daß die von ihnen benutzte Ausrüstung Spitzenqualität hat; die meisten Fotografien jedoch hätten mit recht einfachen Kameras gemacht werden können, ohne daß sich das Ergebnis merkbar von den anderen Aufnahmen unterschieden hätte. Selbstverständlich gibt es Ausnahmen, wenn zum Beispiel Objektive mit äußerst kurzer oder sehr langer Brennweite benutzt werden, um eine außergewöhnliche Perspektive zu erzielen. H.S. Fry, der regelmäßig zum PHOTOGRAPHY YEARBOOK beiträgt, hat letztes Jahr eine Kompaktkamera (des gleichen Typs, der von den meisten Leuten für Urlaubs- und Familienfotos gekauft wird) benutzt anstelle seiner teuren Fotoapparate und Objektive. Mit dieser Kamera erzielte er solch eindrucksvolle Resultate, daß Nikon eine Einzelausstellung mit dem Titel 'Ein Jahr mit einer Kompaktkamera' in ihrer bekannten Galerie veranstaltete.

Hieraus kann man den Schluß ziehen, daß es die Begabung und das Auge des Kamerabenutzers sind, die für die Aufnahme verantwortlich sind, und nicht nur die Kamera. Ich nehme an, daß die meisten Leser dieses Buchs – ich meine diejenigen, die noch nie Beiträge eingeschickt haben – Fotoapparate besitzen, mit denen sie, mit etwas Phantasie, Aufnahmen machen könnten, die dem Niveau der hier veröffentlichten durchaus entsprechen. Geben Sie sich doch mal etwas Mühe! Es besteht sehr wohl die Möglichkeit, daß Ihr Werk in der nächsten Ausgabe veröffentlicht wird – vergessen Sie nicht, es bis zum 31.Januar einzusenden!

Trotz der Tatsache, daß die Originale kleine und große Farbdia sind, sowie unterschiedlich große Schwarzweiß- und Farbabzüge, ist der Verlag sehr um eine hervorragende Qualität der Wiedergabe bemüht. Meiner Meinung nach sind die Reproduktionen manchmal besser als die Originale. Da sich der Verlag dermaßen für die bestmöglichste Wiedergabequalität einsetzt, bitten wir die Einsender darum, dafür zu sorgen, daß ihre Abzüge und Dia keine Unreinheiten haben, daß die Dia keine Kratzer haben, und daß die Aufnahmen gut verpackt abgeschickt werden. Es ist sehr ärgerlich, wenn man ein gutes Dia nicht benutzen kann, weil es einen Kratzer hat, oder einen Abzug nicht, weil er geknickt ist.

Als Herausgeber des PHOTOGRAPHY YEARBOOK möchte ich gemeinsam mit dem Verlag all jenen gratulieren, die zu dieser Ausgabe beigetragen haben, und allen Fotografen danken, die Material eingeschickt haben.

Wie immer hängt die Zukunft des Buchs von denjenigen ab, die Beiträge einschicken; wenn Sie Aufnahmen haben, die sich Ihrer Meinung nach für die nächste Ausgabe eignen (oder wenn Sie andere Fotografen kennen, die geeignete Fotos haben könnten), schicken Sie sie bitte ein vor Ende Januar 1989. Besonders gern sehen wir Material aus dem Ausland, da dadurch der internationale Charakter des Buchs aufrecht erhalten wird.

Farbdia können in beliebiger Größe eingeschickt werden, sie sollten jedoch keinen Glasrahmen haben. Schwarzweiß- und Farbabzüge sollten mindestens 18 x 24cm groß sein, jedoch möglichst nicht größer als 30 x 40cm. Bitte vermerken Sie auf allen Fotoarbeiten den Namen des Fotografen; Angaben zum Aufnahmeort oder Bezeichnung des Motivs; Angaben, die von besonderem Interesse sein könnten; Markenname der Kamera; Brennweite des Objectivs; Filter und das Fabrikat des verwendeten Films. Falls sich die Verpackung zur Rücksendung eignet, und Rückporto oder ein internationaler Antwortschein beigelegt werden, werden die Aufnahmen nach der Auswahl zurückgeschickt, obwohl Fountain Press Limited keine Verantwortung übernimmt für Verluste oder Beschädigungen irgendwelcher Art.

Den erfolgreichen Teilnehmern wird nicht nur das Prestige zuteil, ihre Aufnahmen veröffentlicht zu sehen, zusätzlich erhalten sie eine Ausgabe des PHOTOGRAPHY YEARBOOK und ein Honorar für die Reproduktion.

Das Copyright für jedes veröffentlichte Foto behält der Fotograf.

Wir freuen uns darauf, einige Ihrer Aufnahmen vor Ende Januar 1989 zu sehen.

Peter Wilkinson, FRPS

Comme il arrive depuis de longues années, nombre de bonnes photographies envoyées pour cette édition du PHOTOGRAPHY YEARBOOK n'ont malheureusement pas pu être publiées, faute de place. En procédant à mon choix, je ne regarde pas les noms des auteurs mais les seules oeuvres proposées. Aussi se trouve-t-il parfois que le volume achevé contient plusieurs oeuvres du même photographe, et je comprends la déception de ceux dont les travaux n'ont pas été acceptés. Cependant, le contenu et la présentation du volume doivent être le premier souci de l'éditeur, dût-il y perdre à l'occasion, pour un temps, un ou deux amis!

Mes relations avec la Royal Photographic Society, le London Salon of Photography et le commerce photographique, me conduisent à visiter la plupart des grandes foires commerciales de l'étranger, lesquelles, heureusement, et à la différence des évènements de même nature au Royaume-Uni, comportent presque toujours une section culturelle présentant des photographies. De ce fait, j'ai la chance de voir chaque année des milliers de photographies. Mais cela même ne me donne pas autant de plaisir que le premier coup d'oeil jeté sur les travaux proposés pour le PHOTOGRAPHY YEARBOOK. Ceux-ci nous parviennent de nombreux pays du monde entier. Et comme leurs auteurs appartiennent à toutes sortes de milieux sociaux, et que leur mode de vie et leurs intérêts diffèrent grandement, beaucoup des images qu'ils envoient – soit à cause de leurs sujets, soit à cause des techniques utilisées – sont à la fois originales et particulièrement intéressantes.

Il y a deux remarques que l'on entend souvent – émanant d'un non-photographe admirant une photographie: 'Vous devez avoir un bon appareil' et 'Quel appareil utilisez-vous?'. Pourtant je suis certain que la même personne placée devant l'oeuvre d'un peintre n'irait pas s'enquérir du prix ou de la marque des couleurs ou de la toile utilisées par l'artiste. Les dernières pages de chaque issue du PHOTOGRAPHY YEARBOOK sont consacrées aux 'Informations techniques', simples spécifications relatives à la création des images. Cependant on peut se demander si cette liste des modèles et des marques d'appareils utilisés ne risque pas de contribuer dans une certaine mesure à perpétuer ce mythe qu'il faut un appareil coûteux pour produire une bonne photographie. Le fait que nombre des photographies que nous avons reçues ont été prises par des enthousiastes, amateurs ou professionnels, indique qu'ils se servent très probablement d'un matériel de qualité supérieure, mais en fait la plupart de ces images auraient pu être prises à l'aide d'appareils ordinaires, et les résultats auraient été, pratiquement, à peu près les mêmes. Il y a, naturellement, des cas exceptionnels: par exemple, l'utilisation d'objectifs à très courte ou à tres longue focale peut créer des effets de perspective inattendus. Au cours de l'année passée, M.H.S. Fry, collaborateur régulier du PHOTOGRAPHY YEARBOOK, a utilisé un petit appareil comme ceux dont se servent la plupart des gens qui prennent des instantanés de vacances ou de famille, au lieu de sa coûteuse collection de caméras et d'objectifs. Les résultats qu'il a obtenus avec ce petit appareil ont été tellement remarquables que la compagnie Nikon a organisé dans sa célèbre galerie une exposition intitulée 'One Year with a Compact Camera' consacrée exclusivement à ces photographies.

La morale de cette histoire est que c'est l'oeil et l'intelligence de celui qui utilise l'appareil qui capturent l'image, non pas la seule caméra. Je suppose que la majorité des gens qui verront ce livre – j'entends ceux qui ne sont pas déjà des collaborateurs – possèdent des appareils qui, utilisés avec imagination, pourraient produire des images de la qualité de celles publiées ici. Pourquoi ne pas faire un effort supplémentaire? Vos travaux pourraient être publiés dans notre prochaine édition – mais n'oubliez pas de nous les soumettre avant le 31 janvier.

Bien que les originaux qu'ils reçoivent consistent en un assortiment varié de diapositives, grandes et petites, et d'épreuves, monochromes ou en couleurs de toutes les dimensions, les éditeurs font tout leur possible pour assurer une reproduction de la meilleure qualité. J'estime, en fait, que dans certains cas, la reproduction est meilleure que l'original. Mais puisque les éditeurs font de tels efforts pour assurer la qualité de la reproduction, nous faisons appel à nos collaborateurs pour que, de leur côté, ils prennent soin de nous envoyer des épreuves correctement repiquées, et des diapositives qui ne soient ni rayées ni abimées, et s'assurent que les unes et les autres soient bien emballées avant l'expédition. Il est particulièrement décevant de ne pas pouvoir utiliser une diapositive parcequ'elle est rayée ou une épreuve parce qu'elle est froissée.

En ma capacité de compilateur du PHOTOGRAPHY YEARBOOK, je voudrais me joindre aux éditeurs pour féliciter tous les collaborateurs et remercier tous les photographes qui ont soumis leurs travaux pour cette édition. Comme toujours, l'avenir du livre dépend des collaborateurs. Si vous avez des photographies (ou connaissez d'autres photographes qui en aient), et dont vous estimez qu'elles méritent d'être publiées dans notre prochain numéro, veuillez nous les faire parvenir avant la fin de janvier 1989. Les travaux venant de l'étranger sont particulièrement bienvenus, surtout parce qu'ils contribuent à maintenir le caractère international de notre publication.

Les diapositives peuvent être de n'importe quelles dimensions, mais ne doivent pas être sur verre; les épreuves, monochromes ou en couleurs, doivent mesurer au moins
18 x 24cm, et, autant que possible, ne pas dépasser 30 x 40cm. Toutes les photographies doivent porter le nom de l'auteur ainsi que toutes indications sur le sujet, le lieu où elles ont été prises ou tout autre détail d'un intérêt particulier, la marque de l'appareil, la longueur focale de l'objectif, l'écran et la marque de la pellicule utilisée. Si l'emballage est adéquat, le coût de l'affranchissement ou un coupon-réponse international sont inclus, les travaux soumis seront renvoyés après la sélection, mais Fountain Press Limited ne peut accepter la responsabilité d'aucune perte ou dommages causés aux diapositives ou aux épreuves.

Les collaborateurs dont les travaux auront été acceptés non seulement jouiront du prestige de leur succès, mais recevront chacun un exemplaire du PHOTOGRAPHY YEARBOOK et un cachet comme droit de reproduction. Le copyright de la photographie publiée demeure la propriété de son auteur.

Nous espérons voir quelques unes de vos photographies d'ici la fin de janvier 1989.

Peter Wilkinson, FRPS

Como ha sido usual durante años, se recibieron tantas buenas fotografías para esta edición del PHOTOGRAPHY YEARBOOK, que la falta de espacio hizo imposible la inclusión de muchas de ellas. Cuando hago la selección me limito a observar las fotografías, nunca el nombre de sus autores. Puede por lo tanto ocurrir que, una vez publicado el libro, aparezcan en sus páginas varias fotografías de un mismo autor. Esto, estoy seguro, deberá parecerle frustrante a todos aquellos que enviaron trabajos y que destafortunadamente no fueron seleccionados. Con todo, condisero que el contenido y la composición deben guardar un puesto prioritario dentro de las funciones del editor responsable, aunque esto pueda, en ocasiones, acarrear la pérdida pasajera de una o dos amistades.

Mis vínculos con The Royal Photographic Society, The London Salon of Photography y el mundo fotgráfico en general, me obligan a asistir a las más importantes ferias y exhibiciones en el extranjero, que, afortunadamente, (contrario a lo que ocurre en eventos similares en el Reino Unido) casi siempre tienen secciones culturales en las que exhiben fotografías. Como resultado, tengo el gusto de observar miles de fotografías en el curso de un año. Aún así, la primera ojeada de los trabajos enviados para el PHOTOGRAPHY YEARBOOK, sigue siendo, para mí, *el placer fotográfico del año*. Estas fotografías provienen de muchos países del mundo. Puesto que sus autores son de toda profesión y condición y que por lo tanto poseen intereses variados y distintos, muchas de sus fotografías suelen ser a la vez originales y estimulantes, ya sea por lo inusitado del tema o por la técnica empleada.

Dos frases frecuentes entre los no iniciados al contemplar una fotografía, son las siguientes: "Se necessita una buena cámara" y "?Qué cámara utilizó?". Estoy absolutamente seguro que la misma persona enfrentada a un cuadro, jamás indagaría por el precio o la hechura del lienzo y la pintura utilizados por el artista. Las últimas páginas de cada edición del PHOTOGRAPHY YEARBOOK están destinadas a información técnica, los datos escuetos que contribuyeron en la ejecución de las fotografías. A veces me pregunto si la inclusión de esta lista con los tipos y marcas de las cámaras utilizadas no está perpetuando, de alguna manera, el mito de que es indispensable una cámara costosa para producir buenas fotografías. En este caso, si se tiene en cuenta que casi todos los trabajos fueron realizados por apasionados fotógrafos, trátese de aficionados o profesionales, es muy probable que muchos hayan utilizado equipos altamente sofisticados, pero, de hecho, la mayoría de las fotografías hubieran podido realizarse con cámeras relativamente sencillas y los resultados hubieran sido prácticamente indistinguibles. Existen, por supuesto, excepciones; por ejemplo cuando se utilizaron objetivos de distancia focal muy larga o muy corta para crear perspectivas insólitas. Durante el transcurso del año pasado, un colaborador habitual del PHOTOGRAPHY YEARBOOK, el Sr H.S. Fry, ha venido utilizando una camarita compacta del tipo que la mayoría de la gente utiliza para sus viajes de vacaciones e instantáneas familiares en vez de su extensa colección de cámaras y objetivos costosos. Los resultados fueron tan sorprendentes que Nikon organizó una exhibición individual con sus fotografías en la prestigiosa galería.

La lección que se desprende de esto es que el asunto consiste en ol ojo y la habilidad de la persona que utiliza una cámara para capturar una imagen y no exclusivamente en el tipo de cámara utilizada. Imagino que muchas de las personas que observarán esta publicación, excepción hecha de los que ya colaboraron en ella, disponen de cámaras que, utilizadas con imaginación, serían capaces de producir fotografías de igual calidad a las publicadas. ?Porqué no hacer el esfuerzo? Bien puede suceder que uno de sus trabajos resulte publicado en la próxima edición . . .i No olviden, eso sí, hacer entrega de sus trabajos antes del 31 de enero!

A pesar de que los originales recibidos suelen ser transparencias en color, grandes y pequeñas, copias en positivo de todos los tamaños tanto en blanco y negro como en color, los editores del PHOTOGRAPHY YEARBOOK se esmeran porque las reproducciones sean de la más alta calidad y perfección. Pienso, de hecho, que en algunas oportinidades la reproducción supera el original. Ya que los editores se toman tan en serio el problema de la calidad de las reproducciones, encarecemos la ayuda de los colaboradores asegurándose de que sus copias estén debidamente retocadas, que sus diapositivas no tengan rayones ni manchas y que se cercioren de empacar adecuadamente su trabajo antes de enviarlo. Resulta desalantador no poder usar una buena transparencia porque está rayada o una buena impresión porque venía arrugada.

Como responsable de la edición del PHOTOGRAPHY YEARBOOK, quisiera unir mi voz a las de la casa editora y felicitar a todos los colaboradores así como agradecer a todos los fotógrafos que nos hicieron llegar material para esta publicación.

Como siempre, lo único que garantiza la existencia futura de este anuario son los colaboradores, de manera que si usted posee (o conoce a alguien que posea) material apropiado para la próxima edición, por favor haganoslo llegar antes de finales de enero de 1989. El material proveniente del extranjero será siempre bienvenido, entre otras cosas porque ayuda a mantener el caracter internacional de esta publicación.

Las transparencias en color pueden ser de cualquier tamaño, pero no montadad en vidrio. El tamaño mínimo de las copias en positivo, tanto en blanco y negro como en color, es de 18 – 24 cms y preferiblemente que no excedan los 30 x 40 cms. En todo trabajo debe indicarse el nombre del autor, la información relativa al lugar o sujeto que exhibe, cualquier otro dato de interés general, el tipo de cámara, la distancia focal del objectivo, el filtro y el tipo de película utilizado. Si el empaque es adecuado y se envía el costo postal para su devolución, los trabajos serán devueltos una vez hecha la selección, aunque Fountain Press Limited no se hace responsable por ninguna pérdida o daño que pueda sufrir el material.

Cada fotógrafo seleccionado recibirá, además del prestigio de haber sido incluido en sus páginas, una copia del PHOTOGRAPHY YEARBOOK, así como honorarios por la reproducción. Los derechos de autor de cualquier fotografía publicada permanecerá en manos del mismo.

Esperamos ver algunas de sus fotografías para finales de enero de 1989.

Peter Wilkinson FRPS

Why don't you enjoy the advantages of being a member of The Royal Photographic Society?

JOAN WAKELIN ▷
KENNETH SCOWEN ▽

The Royal Photographic Society is open to *everyone* — young or old, expert or beginner, amateur or professional. If you would like to share your enthusiasm for photography with others equally enthusiastic, then you should seriously consider joining.

Here are just some of the advantages which a member can enjoy:

Membership of the world's leading photographic society.

The opportunity to apply for the Society's distinctions of Licentiateship, Associateship and Fellowship which enable those who qualify to use the letters LRPS, ARPS or FRPS after their name.

'The Photographic Journal', the Society's own monthly magazine, and the bi-monthly 'Journal of Photographic Science'.

Admission to Society meetings anywhere in the world and free admission — together with a guest — to all exhibitions at the RPS National Centre of Photography in Bath.

A well-stocked RPS Bookshop and Mail Order service.

Reduced entrance fees for Society conferences, field trips, weekend instructional workshops, etc., arranged in London, Bath and elsewhere.

Research facilities based on the Society's famous library and collection of photographs and apparatus.

Residential club and restaurant facilities in Central London and preferential accommodation rates in numerous hotels and guest houses in the UK and elsewhere.

Membership of any of the Society's Groups specializing in particular aspects of photography.

Full participation in RPS regional activities.

The right to use the distinctive RPS tie, blazer badge, sweatshirt, wall plaque and other items incorporating the RPS emblem.

The prestige of belonging to a distinguished and learned society — and an impressive Certificate of Membership to prove it.

HEATHER ANGEL △

Anyone may join and there are now nearly 10,000 members all over the world.

Send for full details and a Membership Application form to:

The Secretary
The Royal Photographic Society
RPS National Centre of Photography
The Octagon
Milsom Street
BATH BA1 1DN, UK

Be sure to mark your request 'PYB 1989' in the top left-hand corner and, if you subsequently apply to join the Society, as a reader of the Photographic Yearbook 1989 you will automatically have the normal £10.00 Entrance Fee waived.

THE ROYAL PHOTOGRAPHIC SOCIETY

Patron: Her Majesty Queen Elizabeth II

THE PHOTOGRAPHERS

THE PHOTOGRAPHS

△ KEITH VAUGHAN
◁ W. HARRISON

18

A. McLACHLAN

19

LUCINDA BEATTY △▷

20

PAM GASTON

RICHARD TUCKER △▷

MARK RUSSELL

P. BALDWIN

29

PAM GASTON

DENIS HAYWARD

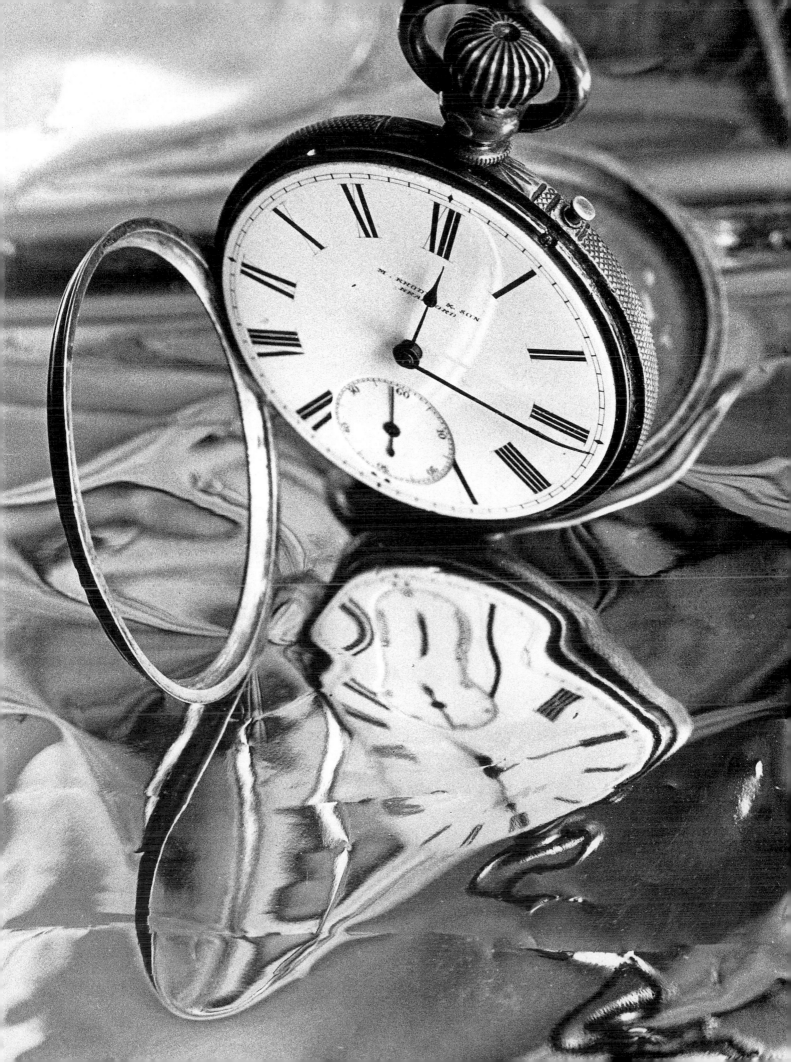

GEORGE HARVEY

W.O. TURNBULL △
DUDLEY WOODS ▷

38

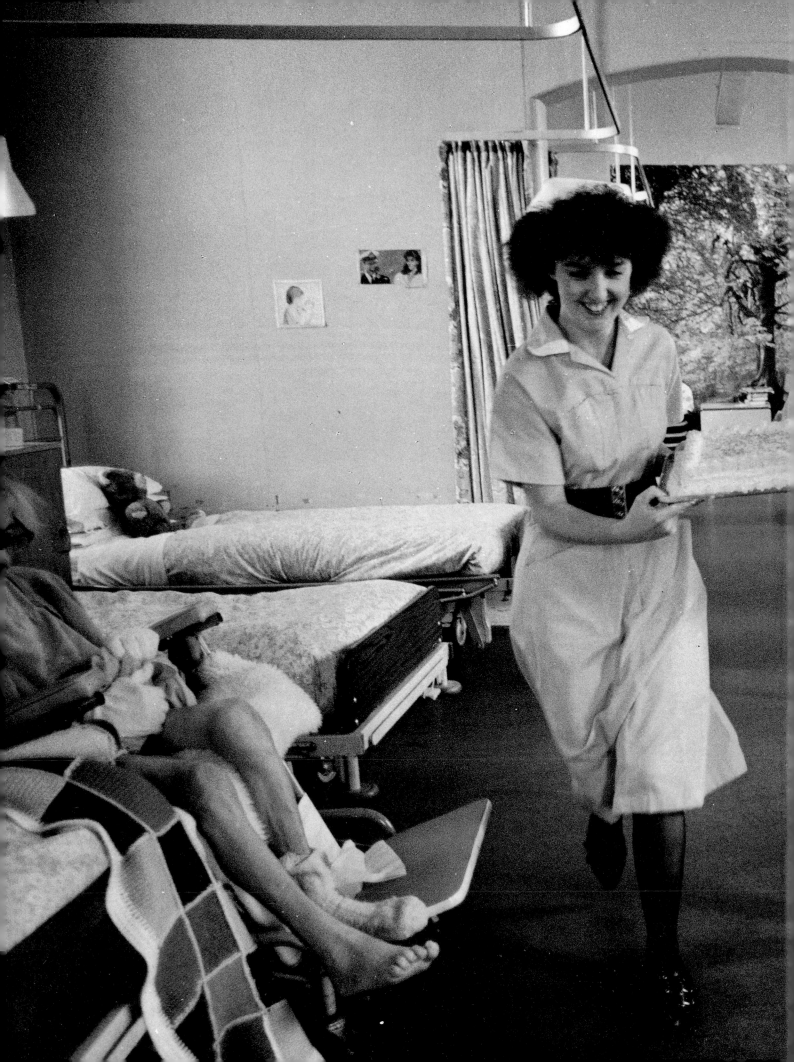

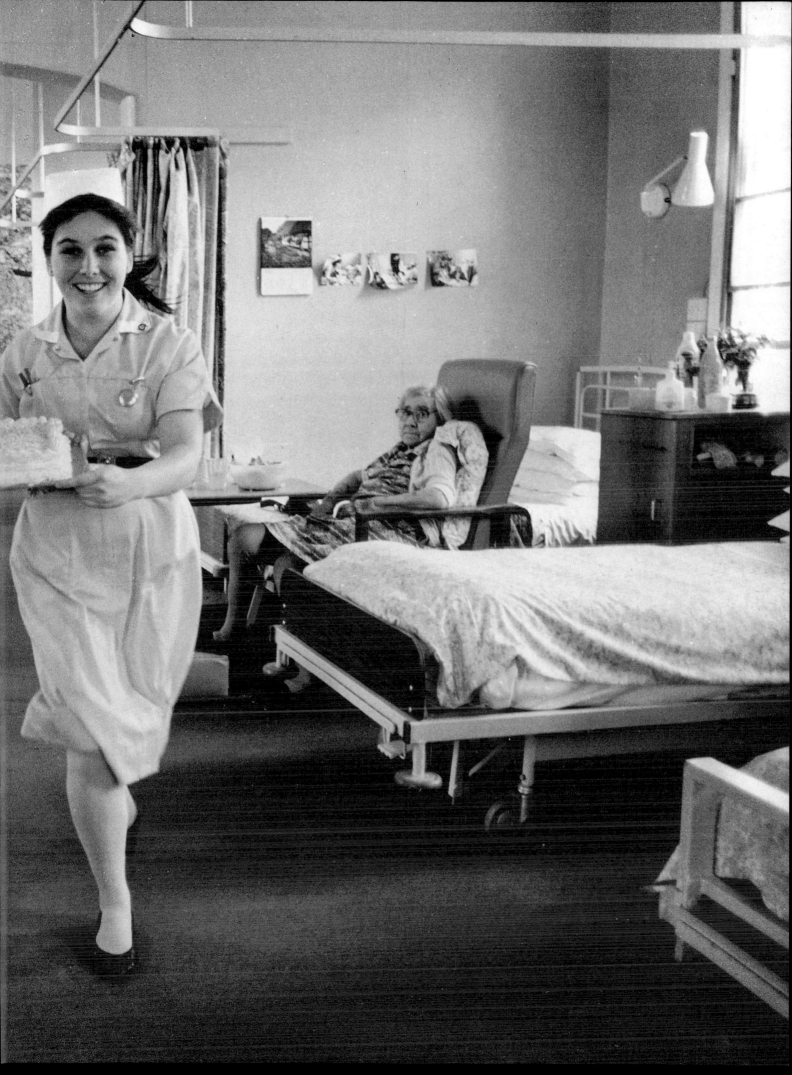

MARTIN FAULKNER △▷
◁ JOAN WAKELIN

42

YGANTIS BRAJIS △
NICK SCOTT ▷

44

◁△ JENIFER ROBERTS

47

△ PAUL ALEXANDER
◁ PETER REES

51

DAVE TOASE △▷

◁ PETER KARRY
△ R. KAWKA
J.C. ABROOK
H.S. FRY ▷

DAVID LANE △▷

58

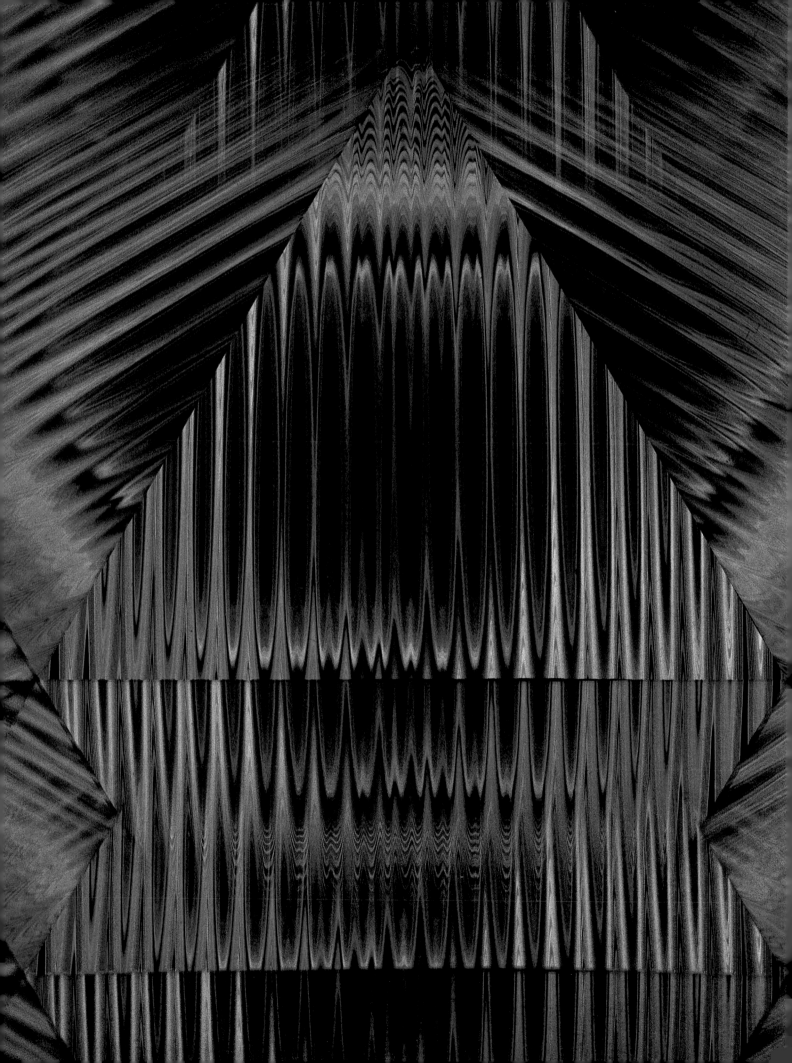

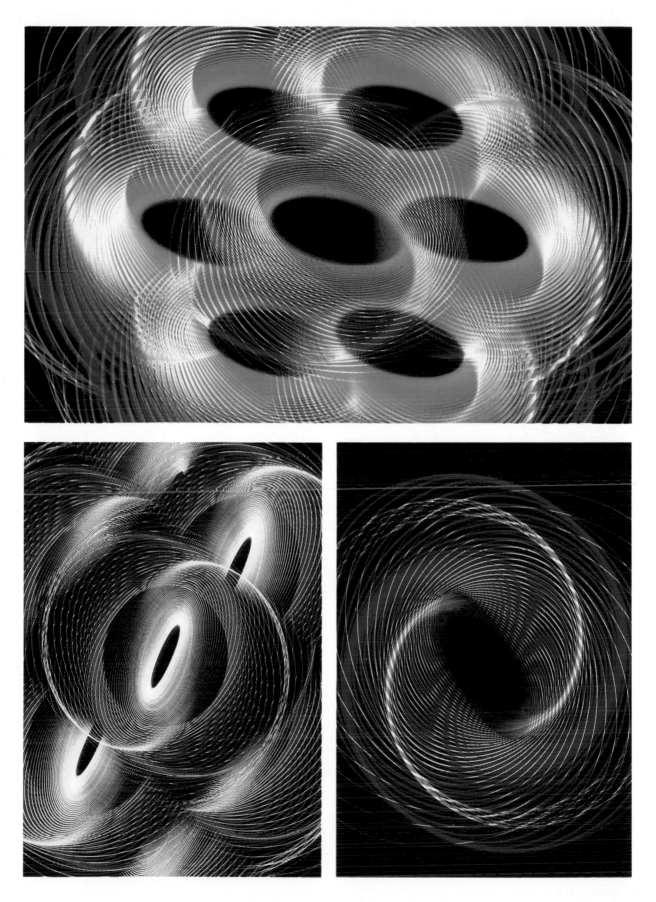

◁△ V. C. NIEMCZYK

61

CARL MASON △
TOM RAFTERY △
E.A.JANES ▷

62

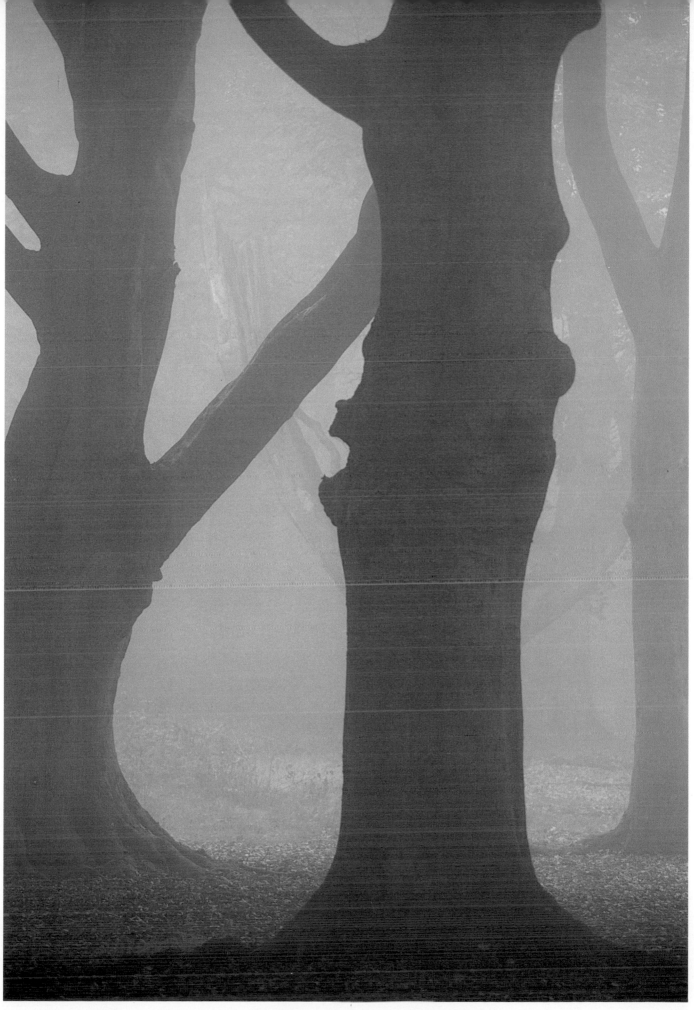

△ GUISEPPE PAPPALARDO
◁ RICHARD BROWN

TOM RICHARDSON △▷

66

STEVE HALE △▷
68

ROBERT ASHBY △▷

70

GEORGE MORRIS △
T. RUDMAN ▷
◁ MIKE HOLLIST

74

MARTIN LANGER △
ROGER FORD ▷

76

△ GEORGE MORRIS
◁ OWEN EVANS

ALAN MILLWARD

△ W.O. TURNBULL
◁ MARK HENNELS

84

△ DENNIS MANSELL
△ MARTIN DEUTSCH
◁ BERT WHALLEY

85

ANDREZEJ SAWA △
ANDREW PERRY ▷

86

OWEN EVANS △
DAVID COOKE ▷
◁ CHING-HSIANG TSAI

90

DENIS HAYWARD

COLIN HARRISON △
D. JOHNSTON ▷
R. SWAIN ▷
◁ GUISEPPE BALLA

98

SHERIF TOMA MIKHAIL ▽▷

J.C. ABROOK △
ANDRZEJ SAWA ▷

102

R. KAWKA △▷

108

IRENE BOOTH △
HARRY AVERY ▷

110

△ E. BOYES
◁ W. TURNBULL

PETER ELGAR △▷

116

JENIFER ROBERTS △▷

△ TONY BOXALL
◁ OWEN EVANS
◁◁ VACLOVAS STRAUKAS

JUOZAS KAZLAUSKAS

124

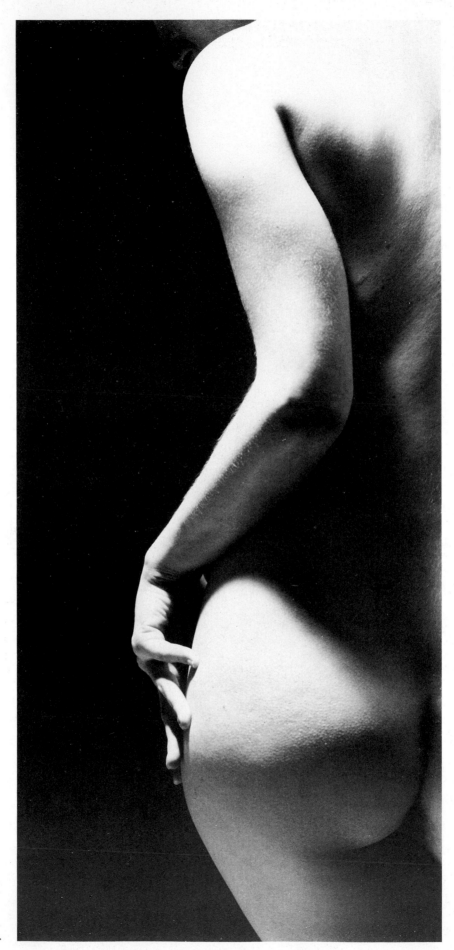

MARK HENNELS △▷

126

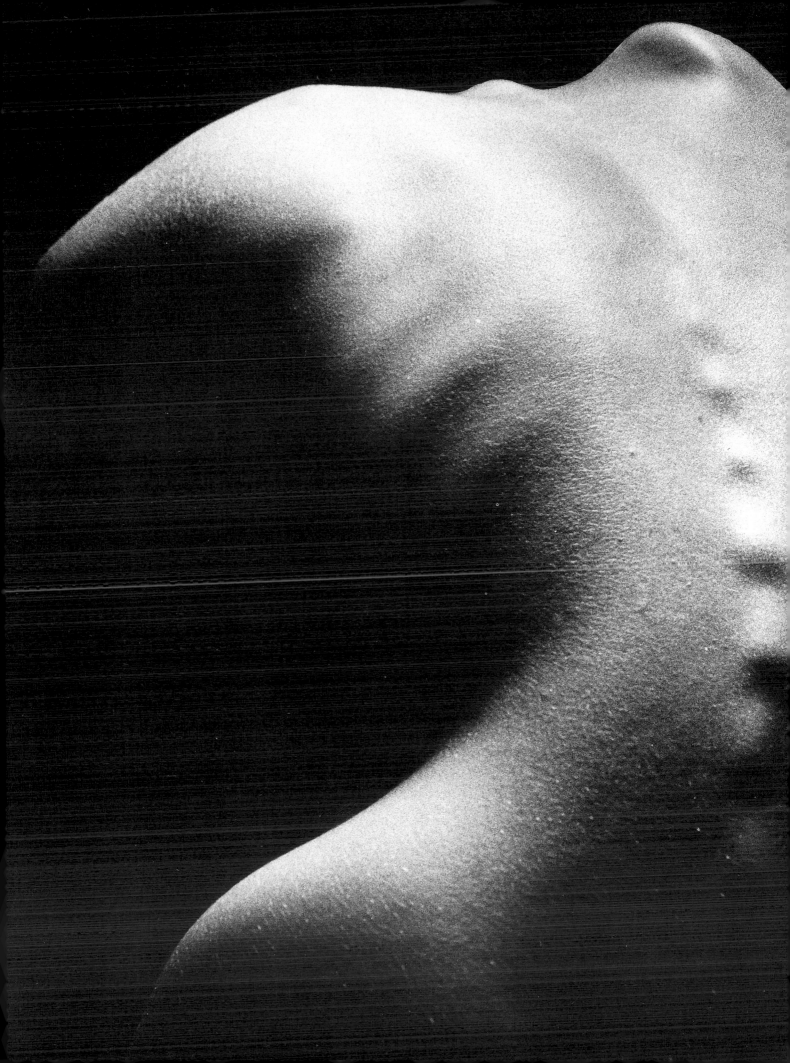

ROMUALDAS POZERSKIS △ ▷

128

130

DENIS HAYWARD

131

△ MARTIN DEUTSCH
◁ MARTIN FAULKNER

133

ALEKSANDRAS MACIJAUSKAS △▷

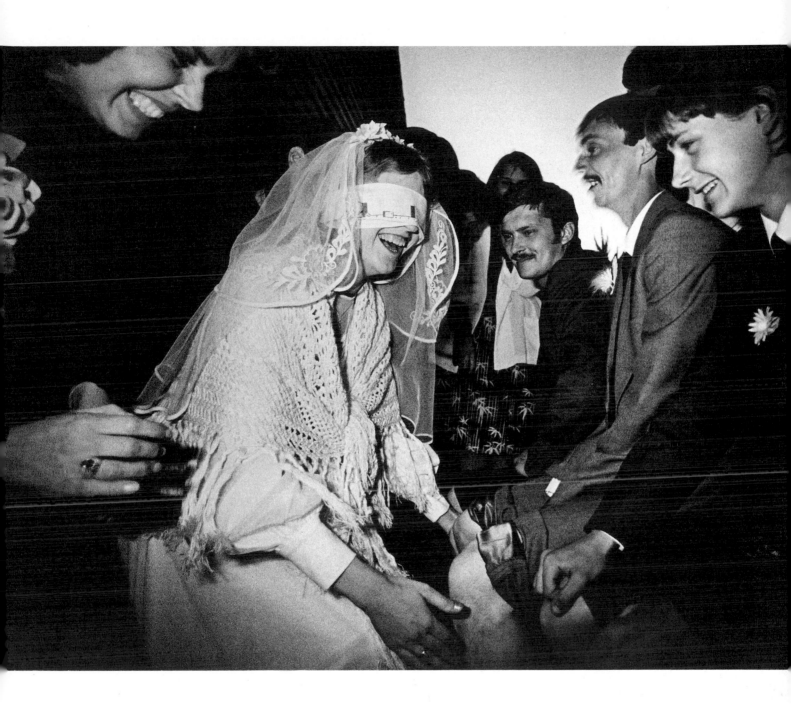

MARK HENNELLS △
HELENE ROGERS ▷

136

R. RAKAUSKAS △
L. BOND ▷

MADAN MOHAN

142

CHRIS ALLEN

143

△ NORMAN LAU
◁ DAVID BOCKING

145

N. MERCER △
ANDRZEJ SAWA ▷

146

J. BEAZLEY △
ANDRZEJ SAWA ▷

148

DAVID JOHNSTON

E. JANES △

AULIS ALEN ▷

154

MICHAEL BENNETT △
KEITH ALLARDYCE ▷
CHRISTOPH RANDLER ▷
RICHARD REVELS ▷

△ MARIPAUS BARANAUSKAS
◁ NORMAN LAU

CAROL STEELE △▷

162

MARTIN DEUTSCH △
DENIS HAYWARD ▷

164

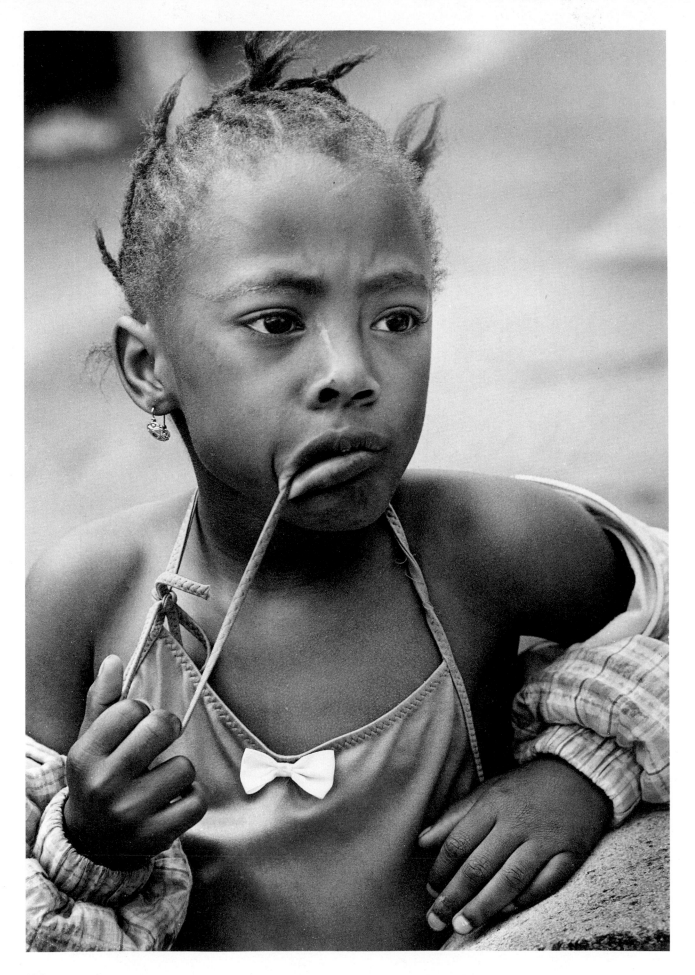

PHILIP ELLIOTT △
DENNIS MANSELL ▷
◁ WILLIAM DOIG

170

△ MIKE BRETT
◁ STANLEY MATCHETT

173

◁ △ PETER KLOPOTOWSKI

LUCILLA PHELPS

176

ROB WILKINSON △
AULIS ALEN ▷

178

RICHARD REVELS △
MICHAEL COOK ▷

180

LO NYIAN LOON

KADIR KABA

◁ MARK RUSSELL

186

△ C. FORSTER
◁ ANDRZEJ SAWA

187

CHRISTIAN HIM ▽▷

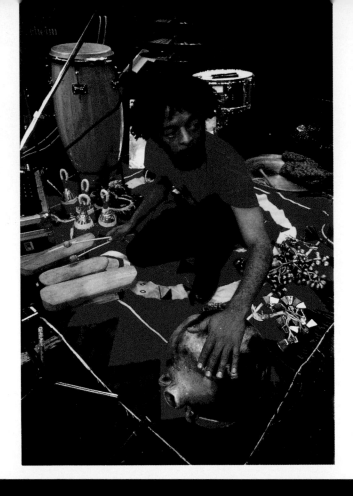

◁△ C.F. BURROWS

191

S. PAUL

192

CHRIS TETTKE

193

DAVID HATFULL △▷
◁ JUOZAS KAZLAUSKAS

196

D. ASHWELL △
JOHN BATTEN ▷

ALAN WISEMAN

MIKE HOLLIST △▷

202

TIM RUDMAN

204

J. DURHAM

205

JOAN WAKELIN △
ALEC PONTON ▷

FUNDRAISING
ACTIVIST MAILING
FINANCES
PERSONNEL

PETER ELGAR △
CASIMIR PUDZIANOWSKI ▷

208

210

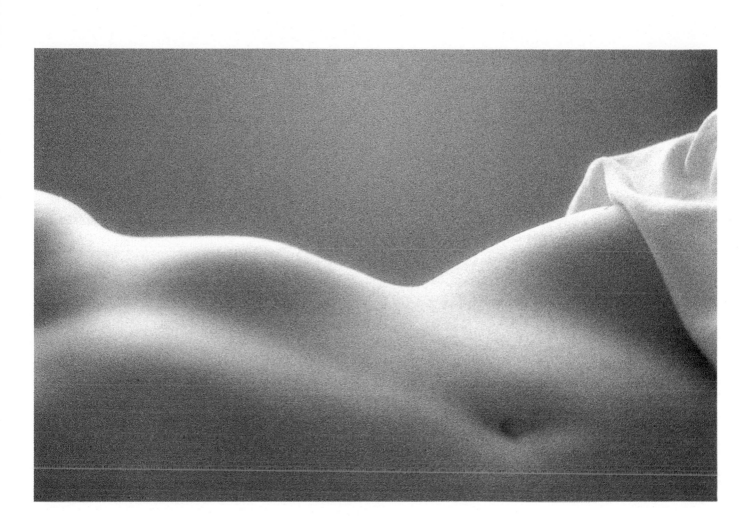

△ P. ALEXANDER
◁ ADRIENNE ROGERS

211

LO NYIAN LOON

212

P. ABIAW △
ALAN BELL ▷
STEVE EATON ▷
KEITH BROWN

DAVID JOHNSTON 216-217 ▷

◁△ PATRICK DUZER

D.P. JOHNSTON

220

PETER WILKINSON

224

TECHNICAL DATA

	Front Endpapers
Photographer	W.O. Turnbull, UK
Location	
Camera	Leica R4
Lens	28mm
Film	Ilford FP4

	17
Photographer	W.T. Harrison, UK
Location	Chelford Steam Rally
Camera	Pentax K2
Lens	85mm
Film	Kodachrome 64

	18
Photographer	Keith Vaughan, Canada
Location	Peggy's Cove, Novia Scotia, Canada
Camera	Canon A1
Lens	70–150mm
Film	Fujichrome 50

	19
Photographer	A.J. McLachlan, UK
Location	Evening Mooring
Camera	Olympus OM2
Lens	24mm
Film	Ektachrome 200

	20 Upper
Photographer	Lucinda Beatty, UK
Location	The Li River, Guangxi, China
Camera	Nikon FE2
Lens	35mm
Film	EPD

	20 Lower
Photographer	Lucinda Beatty, UK
Location	Reed Flute Cave, Guangxi, China
Camera	Nikon FE2
Lens	50mm
Film	EPD

	21
Photographer	Lucinda Beatty, UK
Location	Yangshuo, Guangxi, China
Camera	Nikon FE2
Lens	70mm
Film	EPD

	22
Photographer	Pam Gaston, UK
Location	Swan Portrait
Camera	Nikon FM2
Lens	300mm
Film	Kodachrome 64

	23
Photographer	E.A. Janes, UK
Location	Mute Swan at Sunset, Tring
Camera	Olympus OM2
Lens	35–70mm Zoom
Film	Kodachrome 64

	24–25
Photographer	Keith Vaughan, Canada
Location	Hoar Frost Mist, Halifax Harbour, Nova Scotia, Canada
Camera	Canon A1
Lens	70–150mm Zoom
Film	Fujichrome 50

	26
Photographer	Richard Tucker, UK
Location	Iceland
Camera	Nikon F3
Lens	16mm
Film	Kodachrome 64

	27
Photographer	Richard Tucker, UK
Location	Iceland
Camera	Nikon F3
Lens	16mm
Film	Kodachrome 64

	28
Photographer	Mark Russell, UK
Location	Temple of Heaven, Beijing, China
Camera	OM2N
Lens	50mm
Film	Kodachrome 64

	29
Photographer	P.E. Baldwin, UK
Location	Lanchou, China
Camera	Nikon FA
Lens	28–85mm Zoom
Film	Kodachrome 64

	30
Photographer	Pam Gaston, UK
Location	
Camera	Nikon FM2
Lens	50mm
Film	Fujichrome 100

	31
Photographer	Denis Hayward, UK
Location	Bullseal Elephant, Falkland Islands
Camera	Nikon F3
Lens	35–105mm Zoom
Film	Kodachrome 100

	32
Photographer	C. O'Connor, UK
Location	The Sundial, St Katherine's Dock, London
Camera	OM2N
Lens	24mm Polaroid Filter
Film	Agfa

	33
Photographer	E. Boyes, UK
Location	Reflections in Time
Camera	Yashica AX
Lens	Zoom
Film	Ilford FP4

	34
Photographer	George Harvey (Royal Navy Photographer), UK
Location	Nuclear Submarine HMS Courageous
Camera	Hasselblad 500
Lens	100mm
Film	Ilford HP5

	35
Photographer	Phil Ball (Royal Navy Photographer), UK
Location	Nuclear-Powered Submarine HMS Trafalgar Heads for the Atlantic
Camera	Hasselblad 500
Lens	80mm
Film	Ilford FP4

	36
Photographer	David Mansell, UK
Camera	Nikon
Lens	35mm
Film	Kodak Tri-X

37

Photographer — Asadour Guzelian, UK
Location — Alicia Markova taking a Ballet Class at Ilkley, Yorkshire
Camera — Nikon FM2
Lens — 180mm
Film — Kodak Tri-X

38

Photographer — W.O. Turnbull, UK
Location — Winchester Hill
Camera — Leica R4
Lens — 28mm
Film — Ilford FP4

39

Photographer — Dudley Woods, UK
Location — The Magic Circle, Rollright Stones, Oxfordshire
Camera — Olympus OM1
Lens — 25mm
Film — Ilford FP4

40–41

Photographer — Joan Wakelin, UK
Location — Birthday Party at Geriatric Hospital
Camera — Canon AE1
Lens — 24mm
Film — Ilford XP1

42

Photographer — Martin Faulkner, UK
Location — Notting Hill, London
Camera — Canon A1
Lens — 85mm
Film — Ilford XP1

43

Photographer — Martin Faulkner, UK
Location — Notting Hill, London
Camera — Canon A1
Lens — 85mm
Film — Ilford XP1

44

Photographer — Vjgantas Brajis, Lithuania/USSR
Location — Building Construction
Camera — Kiev 88
Lens — Zodiak
Film —

45

Photographer — Nick Scott, UK
Location — York Station
Camera — Hasselblad
Lens — 80mm
Film — Ilford FP4

46

Photographer — Jennifer Roberts, UK
Location — Luxor, Upper Egypt
Camera — Olympus OM1
Lens — 100mm
Film — Kodak Tri-X

47

Photographer — Jenifer Roberts, UK
Location — Sunrise, Southern Italy
Camera — Olympus OM2
Lens — 80–210mm Zoom
Film — Kodak Tri-X

48

Photographer — Nigel Wiggelsworth, UK
Location — Leeds Castle – Hot Air Balloon
Camera — Nikon FE2
Lens — 24mm
Film — Ilford HP5

49

Photographer — Chris North (Royal Navy Photographer), UK
Location — Frigate HMS Minerva and Stingray Torpedo-armed Lynx Helicopter in Force 9 Gale
Camera — Hasselblad 2000
Lens — 80mm
Film — Kodak VR400

50

Photographer — Peter Rees, UK
Location — Summer Glade
Camera — Olympus OM1N
Lens — 70–150mm Zoom
Film — Ektachrome

51

Photographer — Paul Alexander, UK
Location — Woodland in Derbyshire
Camera — Olympus OM1
Lens — 50mm
Film — Kodachrome 64

52

Photographer — Dave Toase, UK
Location — Garry Culshaw on Stage at Band On The Wall, Manchester
Camera — Minolta X700
Lens — 35–210mm Zoom
Film — Fujichrome 1600

53

Photographer — Dave Toase, UK
Location — Viv Dixon on Stage at The International, Manchester
Camera — Minolta X700
Lens — 35–100mm Zoom
Film — Kodachrome 800

54

Photographer — Peter Karry, UK
Location — Beresford Dale
Camera — Mamiya 645
Lens — 80mm
Film —

55 Upper

Photographer — R. Kawka, UK
Location — Bridell, Dyfed, Wales
Camera — Yashicamat
Lens — 80mm
Film — Kodachrome 64

55 Lower

Photographer — J.C. Abrook, UK
Location — Lake District
Camera — Pentax LX
Lens — 100mm
Film — Kodachrome 25

56–57

Photographer — H.S. Fry, UK
Location — Dal Lake, Kashmir
Camera — Nikon F3
Lens — 80–200mm Zoom
Film — Kodachrome 200

58

Photographer — David Lane, UK
Location — Robin, Wallsend
Camera — Mamiya RZ67
Lens — 180mm
Film — Fujichrome 100

59
Photographer David Lane, UK
Location Chaffinch, Wooler, Northumberland
Camera Mamiya RZ67
Lens 180mm
Film Fujichrome 100

60 and 61
Photographer V.C. Niemczyk, UK
Location Abstracts
Camera Canon AEI
Lens 50mm
Film Ektacolor 160

62 Upper
Photographer Carl Mason, UK
Location Shades of Green Northwood, Middlesex
Camera Nikon FE
Lens 200mm
Film Kodachrome 64

62 Lower
Photographer Tom Raftery, Eire
Location Bluebells and Beech Trees, Boyle, County Roscommon
Camera Canon A1
Location 28mm
Film Kodachrome 25

63
Photographer E.A. Janes, UK
Location Frithsden Beeches, Ashridge Park, Herts
Camera Olympus OM2
Lens 35–70mm Zoom
Film Kodachrome 64

64
Photographer Richard Brown, UK
Location Self Portrait
Camera Nikon FE
Lens 28mm
Film Kodachrome 100

65
Photographer Guiseppe Pappalardo, Italy
Location Old-Fashioned Home in Catania, Sicily
Camera Hasselblad
Lens 50mm
Film Ilford FP4

66
Photographer Tom Richardson, UK
Location Scotland
Camera Minolta SRT101
Lens 28mm
Film Agfapan 100

67
Photographer Tom Richardson, UK
Location Port Appin, Loch Linhe, Argyll, Scotland
Camera Minolta SRT303
Lens 28mm
Film Agfapan 100

68
Photographer Steve Hale, UK
Location Wimbledon Ball Girl
Camera Nikon F3
Lens 135mm
Film Kodak Tri-X

69
Photographer Steve Hale, UK
Location Bruce Grobbelaar, Liverpool FC Goalkeeper
Camera Nikon
Lens 400mm
Film Ilford XP1

70 and 71
Photographer Robert Ashby, UK
Location Pilgrims of Croagh, Patrick, County Mayo
Camera Canon AE1
Lens 50mm
Film Kodak Tri-X

72–73
Photographer Mike Hollist, UK
Location Metropolitan Police Horse Riders at their Annual Horse Show in London
Camera Nikon F2
Lens 300mm
Film Kodak Tri-X

74
Photographer George Morris, UK
Location Greenhouses, Hawkshead
Camera Nikon FE
Lens 28mm
Film Ilford XP1

75
Photographer Tim Rudman, UK
Location
Camera Yashica SLR
Lens 35mm
Film Ilford FP4

76
Photographer Martin Langer, W. Germany
Location
Camera
Lens
Film

77
Photographer Roger Ford, UK
Location Double Header, Monks Orchard Gym, Croydon
Camera Minolta X700
Lens 75–150mm Zoom
Film Ilford HP5

78
Photographer Owen Evans, UK
Location Winter Evening, Dwynyd Estuary
Camera Pentax Spotmatic
Lens 24mm
Film Ilford FP4

79
Photographer George Morris, UK
Location
Camera Nikon FE
Lens 28mm
Film Ilford XP1

80
Photographer Alan Millward, Canada
Location Hindu Child
Camera Pentax K1000
Lens 500mm
Film Kodak Tri-X

81
Photographer Giuseppe Pappalardo, Italy
Location Tokyo
Camera Hasselblad
Lens 80mm
Film Kodak Tri-X

82
Photographer · Mark Hinnells, UK
Location · Track Fence, Loughborough University
Camera · Nikon F3
Lens · 50mm
Film · Kodak Tri-X

83
Photographer · W.O. Turnbull, UK
Location · Tyre Tracks
Camera · Leica R4
Lens · 28mm
Film · Ilford FP4

84
Photographer · Bert Whalley, UK
Location · Walkers on Fairfield, Cumbria
Camera · Yashica 124G
Lens · Orange Filter
Film · Ilford

85 Upper
Photographer · Dennis Mansell, UK
Location · Brecon Beacons, South Wales
Camera · Hasselblad
Lens · 50mm
Film · Kodak Tri-X

85 Lower
Photographer · Martin Deutsch, USA
Location · A Walk in the Snow
Camera · Olympus OM1
Lens · 27mm
Film · Ilford FP4

86
Photographer · Andrzej Sawa, South Africa
Location · Beach Shadow, Malawi
Camera · Nikon FA
Lens · 24mm
Film ·

87
Photographer · Andrew Perry, UK
Location ·
Camera · Canon F1
Lens · 50mm
Film · Agfapan 100

89–89
Photographer · Ching-Hsiang Tsai, Taiwan
Location ·
Camera ·
Lens ·
Film ·

90
Photographer · Owen Evans, UK
Location ·
Camera · Pentax MX
Lens · 200mm
Film · Ilford HP5

91
Photographer · David Cooke, UK
Location ·
Camera · Nikon F3AF
Lens · 200mm
Film · Kodak Tri-X

92–93
Photographer · Denis Hayward, UK
Location · Grytviken Harbour, Falklands
Camera · Hasselblad
Lens · 80mm
Film · Ilford FP4

94
Photographer · Christian Him, France
Location · Horace Silver at Ronnie Scott's Club
Camera · Olympus OM2
Lens · 135mm
Film · Kodak T Max

95
Photographer · Christian Him, France
Location · Art Blakey at The Shaw Theatre
Camera · Olympus OM2
Lens · 50mm
Film · Kodak T Max

96
Photographer · William Doig, UK
Location · Water Skiing – MacDuff Harbour, Banffshire, Scotland
Camera · Mamiyaflex C330
Lens · 180mm
Film · Ilford FP4

97
Photographer · Guiseppe Balla, Italy
Location · Sulla Cresta
Camera · Canon F1
Lens · 70–150mm Zoom
Film · Ektachrome 64

98
Photographer · Colin Harrison, UK
Location · Night Departure
Camera · Pentax Spotmatic
Lens · 50mm
Film · Kodachrome 64

99 Upper
Photographer · David Johnston, UK
Location · Severn Valley Railway, Bewdley
Camera · Leica R4S
Lens · 90mm
Film · Kodak

99 Lower
Photographer · R.W.A. Swain, UK
Location · Steamtown, Carnforth
Camera · Canon AEI
Lens · 28mm
Film · Kodachrome 64

100–101
Photographer · Sherif T. Mikhail, Egypt
Location · Underwater Red Sea
Camera · Nikonos V
Lens · Flash
Film · Kodachrome 100

102
Photographer · J.C. Abrook, UK
Location · Painted Miss, Covent Garden, London
Camera · Pentax LX
Lens · 70–210mm Zoom
Film · Kodachrome 200

103
Photographer · Andrzej Sawa, South Africa
Location · Painted Face
Camera · Nikon FA
Lens · 105mm
Film · Fujichrome 100

	104–105
Photographer	Lucilla Phelps, UK
Location	Cambridge Blue at Henley
Camera	Nikon
Lens	300mm
Film	VP3

	106
Photographer	Alistair McIntosh, UK
Location	Trafalgar Square, London
Camera	Pentax MX
Lens	80–200mm Zoom
Film	Kodachrome 100

	107
Photographer	Colin Harrison, UK
Location	Hot Air
Camera	Canon AEI
Lens	50mm
Film	Kodachrome 64

	108
Photographer	R. Kawka, UK
Location	Sulphur Tuft, Maulden Woods, Bedfordshire
Camera	Yashica 635
Lens	Close Up
Film	Fujichrome 50

	109
Photographer	R. Kawka, UK
Location	Common Earth Ball, Maulden Woods, Bedfordshire
Camera	Yashica 635
Lens	Close Up
Film	Fujichrome 50

	110
Photographer	Irene Booth, UK
Location	Wengen, Switzerland
Camera	Praktica MTL5
Lens	50mm
Film	Agfa CT18

	111
Photographer	Harry Avery, UK
Location	Winter Sunshine
Camera	Leicaflex
Lens	50mm
Film	Kodak Ektachrome

	112
Photographer	Richard Brown, UK
Location	Shannon Bridge, Ireland
Camera	Nikon FM
Lens	35mm
Film	Kodachrome 64

	113
Photographer	Tony Boxall, UK
Location	Sealyham Dogs
Camera	Mamiya C330
Lens	80mm
Film	Kodak Tri-X

	114
Photographer	W.O. Turnbull, UK
Location	Complementary Verticals
Camera	Leica R4
Lens	135mm
Film	Ilford FP4

	115
Photographer	E. Boyes, UK
Location	A Bay near Portmadoc, Wales
Camera	Yashica AX 35mm
Lens	28–80mm Zoom
Film	Ilford FP4

	116–117
Photographer	Peter Elgar
Location	Calgary Stampede
Camera	Pentax LX
Lens	300mm
Film	Ilford XP1

	118
Photographer	Jenifer Roberts, UK
Location	Old Bakawal Woman in Kashmir
Camera	Olympus OM2
Lens	85–210mm Zoom
Film	Kodak Tri-X

	119
Photographer	Jenifer Roberts, UK
Location	A Dard Village in Kashmir
Camera	Olympus OM2
Lens	85–210mm Zoom
Film	Kodak Tri-X

	120–121
Photographer	Vaclovas Straukas, Lithuania/USSR
Location	Morning
Camera	Zorky
Lens	Industar Lens
Film	Agfa

	122
Photographer	Owen Evans, UK
Location	
Camera	Pentax MX
Lens	200mm
Film	Ilford FP4

	123
Photographer	Tony Boxall, UK
Location	Old Bargee in Birmingham
Camera	Mamiya C330
Lens	80mm
Film	Kodak Tri-X

	124 and 125
Photographer	Juozas Kazlauskas, Lithuania/USSR
Location	Following the Traces of Lost Polar Expeditions
Camera	
Lens	
Film	

	126
Photographer	Mark Hinnells, UK
Location	Gentle Lines
Camera	Bronica
Lens	200mm
Film	Kodak T Max

	127
Photographer	Mark Hinnells, UK
Location	
Camera	Nikon FM2
Lens	50mm Vivitar
Film	Kodak Plus-X

	128–129
Photographer	Romualdas Pozerskis, Lithuania/USSR
Location	Country Celebrations
Camera	Minolta XD 11
Lens	24mm
Film	KN3

130–131
Photographer Denis Hayward, UK
Location Grytviken, South Georgia, Falklands
Camera Hasselblad
Lens 80mm
Film Ilford FP4

132
Photographer Martin Faulkner, UK
Location Rue St Sauveur, Paris
Camera Canon A1
Lens 85mm
Film Agfapan 400

133
Photographer Martin Deutsch, USA
Location New York City
Camera Olympus
Lens 50mm
Film

134–135
Photographer Aleksandras Macijauskas, Lithuania/USSR
Location
Camera Nikon F
Lens 24mm
Film Foto 250

136
Photographer Mark Hinnells, UK
Location Snowstorm, Rushup Edge, Edale
Camera Bronica ETRS
Lens 75mm
Film Kodak T Max

137
Photographer Helene Rogers, UK
Location Fjord, Iceland
Camera Canon F1
Lens 17mm
Film Ilford XP1

138
Photographer Clive Harrison, UK
Location Notting Hill Carnival, London
Camera Olympus OM1N
Lens 100mm
Film Ilford XP1

139
Photographer Clive Harrison, UK
Location Base Clarinet Player, Clerkenwell Green, London
Camera Olympus OM1N
Lens 28mm
Film Ilford XP1

140
Photographer Romualdas Rakauskas, Lithuania/USSR
Location
Camera Praktica LTL
Lens 50mm
Film NK2

141
Photographer L. Bond, UK
Location Family Sleigh Ride
Camera Canon A1
Lens 135mm
Film Ilford HP5

142
Photographer Madan Mohan, India
Location Delhi, India
Camera Agfa Isolette III
Lens 120mm
Film Agfa 125

143
Photographer Chris Allen, UK
Location
Camera Pentax MX
Lens 50mm
Film Kodak T Max

144
Photographer David Bocking, UK
Location Chinese Takeaway, West Bowling, Bradford
Camera Olympus OM1
Lens 24mm
Film Kodak Tri-X

145
Photographer Norman Lau, Hong Kong
Location
Camera Hasselblad
Lens 150mm
Film Kodak

146
Photographer N. Mercer, UK
Location Wreck of Sailing Coaster 'Louise', Grytviken, South Georgia, Falklands
Camera Miranda
Lens 80–200mm Zoom
Film Kodak Gold

147
Photographer Andrzej Sawa, South Africa
Location Malawi
Camera Nikon FA
Lens 20mm
Film Fujichrome 100

148
Photographer Jeffrey Beazley, UK
Location Near Tittensor, Staffordshire
Camera Pentax MX
Lens 100mm
Film Fujichrome 100

149
Photographer Andrzej Sawa, South Africa
Location Blue Landscape
Camera Nikon FA
Lens
Film

150
Photographer David Johnston, UK
Location Alexander Stadium, Birmingham
Camera Leica R4S
Lens 135mm
Film Kodak

151
Photographer Peter Symes, UK
Location Hiram Bullock
Camera Nikon FE
Lens 80–200mm Zoom
Film Kodachrome 400

152-153

Photographer	David Johnston, UK
Location	Handsworth, Birmingham
Camera	Leica R4S
Lens	90mm
Film	Kodachrome

154

Photographer	E.A. Janes, UK
Location	Ashridge, Hertfordshire
Camera	Olympus OM2
Lens	28mm
Film	Kodachrome 64

155

Photographer	Aulis Alen, New Zealand
Location	Himalayan Tahr in Wellington, New Zealand
Camera	Pentax
Lens	200mm
Film	Kodak Ektachrome

156

Photographer	Michael Bennett, UK
Location	
Camera	Nikon FA
Lens	70-210mm Zoom
Film	

157 Upper

Photographer	Keith Allardyce, UK
Location	Gannet over the Bass Rock, Scotland
Camera	Nikkormat FT2
Lens	300mm
Film	Kodachrome 64

157 Middle

Photographer	Christoph Randler, West Germany
Location	
Camera	Nikon FA
Lens	400mm
Film	Kodachrome 64

157 Lower

Photographer	Richard Revels, UK
Location	Arctic Tern
Camera	Canon A1
Lens	35-70mm Zoom
Film	Ektachrome 200

158

Photographer	Richard Revels, UK
Location	Larva of Death Head Hawk Moth
Camera	Canon T90
Lens	100mm
Film	Kodachrome 64

159

Photographer	Richard Revels, UK
Location	Puss Moth Larva
Camera	Canon T90
Lens	100mm
Film	Kodachrome 64

160

Photographer	Norman Lau, Hong Kong
Location	Father and Child
Camera	Hasselblad
Lens	150mm
Film	Kodak

161

Photographer	Marjonas Baranauskas, Lithuania/USSR
Location	Fisherman
Camera	Mamiya
Lens	80mm
Film	Foto 65

162

Photographer	Carol Steele, UK
Location	
Camera	Pentax ME Super
Lens	24mm, Wratten 29 Filter
Film	Kodak High Speed Infra Red Film

163

Photographer	Carol Steele, UK
Location	Cockington Woods, Torquay, South Devon
Camera	Pentax ME Super
Lens	24mm Wratten 87 Filter
Film	Kodak High Speed Infra Red Film

164

Photographer	Martin Deutsch, USA
Location	Fire in Jersey City, New Jersey, USA
Camera	Olympus OM1N
Lens	24mm
Film	Kodak Plus X

165

Photographer	Denis Hayward, UK
Location	Fire Practice in Northern Ireland
Camera	Hasselblad
Lens	80mm
Film	Ilford HP5

166

Photographer	Clive Harrison, UK
Location	Notting Hill
Camera	Olympus OM1N
Lens	100mm
Film	Ilford XP1

167

Photographer	Clive Harrison, UK
Location	Girl at Hammersmith Bridge Centenary Celebration
Camera	Olympus OM1N
Lens	100mm
Film	Ilford XP1

168-169

Photographer	William Doig, UK
Location	
Camera	Minolta Autocord
Lens	
Film	Kodak Tri-X

170

Photographer	Philip Elliott, UK
Location	Beach in Pembrokeshire
Camera	Olympus OM1
Lens	21mm
Film	Ilford FP4

171

Photographer	Denis Mansell, UK
Location	Zillertal, Austria
Camera	Nikon
Lens	50mm
Film	Kodak Tri-X

172

Photographer	Stanley Matchett, UK
Location	
Camera	Nikon F3
Lens	200mm
Film	Ilford HP5

173
Photographer — Mike Brett, UK
Location — Great Britain vs. Papua New Guinea (Rugby League) International
Camera — Nikon FM2
Lens — 300mm
Film — Kodak T Max

174
Photographer — Peter Klopotowski, Australia
Location —
Camera — Nikon F2
Lens — 24mm
Film — Kodak Tri-X

175
Photographer — Peter Klopotowski, Australia
Location —
Camera — Rolleiflex
Lens — 80mm
Film — Kodak Tri-X

176
Photographer — Lucilla Phelps, UK
Location — Octagon at Orleans House Gallery
Camera — Nikon
Lens — 6mm
Film — Ilford FP4

177
Photographer — John Parker (Royal Navy Photographer), UK
Location — Arctic Lights
Camera — Hasselblad 500
Lens — 80mm
Film — Kodak VPS 3

178
Photographer — Rob Wilkinson, UK
Location — Vancouver City at Dusk
Camera — Mamiya 300F
Lens — 80mm
Film — Fujichrome 100

179
Photographer — Aulis Alen, New Zealand
Location — Daybreak, Wellington Harbour, New Zealand
Camera — Pentax
Lens — 200mm
Film — Kodak Ektachrome

180
Photographer — Richard Revels, UK
Location — Stinging Nettle Stings
Camera — Canon T90
Lens — 35mm, Electronic Flash
Film — Kodachrome 64

181
Photographer — Michael Cook, UK
Location — Poppy Head
Camera — Nikon FA
Lens — 35–200mm Zoom
Film — Ektachrome 100

182
Photographer — Lo Nyian Loon, Sarawack
Location — Sibuti, Malaysia
Camera — Nikon FM
Lens — 105mm
Film —

183
Photographer — Kadir Kaba, Turkey
Location — Turkey
Camera — Olympus OM1
Lens — 85mm
Film — Agfa CT18

184–185
Photographer — Mark Russell, UK
Location — Wall of Forbidden City, Beijing, China
Camera — Olympus OM2N
Lens — 28mm
Film — Kodachrome 64

186
Photographer — Andrzej Sawa, South Africa
Location —
Camera — Nikon FA
Lens — 35–200mm Zoom
Film — Fujichrome 100

187
Photographer — Chris Forster, UK
Location — Entertainments Centre, Milton Keynes
Camera — Pentax MX
Lens — 24–35mm with Polarizing Filter
Film — Kodachrome 25

188 Upper
Photographer — Christian Him, France
Location — Nana Vasconselos
Camera — Olympus OM2
Lens — 24mm
Film — Kodachrome 160

188 Lower
Photographer — Christian Him, France
Location — Alice Coltrane
Lens — 135mm
Film — Kodachrome 160

189 Upper
Photographer — Christian Him, France
Location — Gil Evans
Camera — Olympus OM1
Lens — 135mm
Film — Kodachrome 400

189 Lower
Photographer — Christian Him, France
Location — Hermeto Pascoal
Camera — Olympus OM1
Lens — 200mm
Film — Kodachrome 160

190
Photographer — C.F. Burrows, UK
Location — Sweets
Camera — Chinon CE4
Lens — Standard
Film — Fujichrome 50

191
Photographer — C.F. Burrows, UK
Location — Crayon Shavings
Camera — Chinon CE4
Lens — Standard
Film — Fujichrome 100

192
Photographer — S. Paul, India
Location —
Camera —
Lens —
Film —

193
Photographer — Chris Tettke, West Germany
Location —
Camera —
Lens —
Film —

194–195

Photographer	Juozas Kazlauskas Lithuania/USSR
Location	
Camera	Canon
Lens	80mm
Film	Foto 65

196

Photographer	David Hatfull, UK
Location	
Camera	Pentax
Lens	20mm
Film	Ilford HP5

197

Photographer	David Hatfull, UK
Location	
Camera	Canon F1
Lens	20mm
Film	Kodak Tri-X

198

Photographer	D. Ashwell, UK
Location	
Camera	Olympus OM1
Lens	28mm
Film	Kodak Tri-X

199

Photographer	John Batten, UK
Location	
Camera	Leicaflex SL2
Lens	24mm
Film	Kodak Tri-X

200–201

Photographer	Alan Wiseman, UK
Location	L'Apres Midi (Serpentine)
Camera	Olympus OM1N
Lens	85mm
Film	Kodak High Speed Infra Red Film

202

Photographer	Mike Hollist, UK
Location	Owls at Surrey Bird Rescue Centre
Camera	Nikon F2
Lens	180mm
Film	Kodak Tri-X

203

Photographer	Mike Hollist, UK
Location	Layang Layang, Baby Indian Elephant at London
Camera	Nikon F2
Lens	180mm
Film	Kodak Tri-X

204

Photographer	Tim Rudman, UK
Location	
Camera	Yashica 35
Lens	24mm
Film	Ilford FP4

205

Photographer	J. Durham, UK
Location	
Camera	Canon F1
Lens	24mm
Film	Ilford FP4

206

Photographer	Joan Wakelin, UK
Location	Greenham Common
Camera	Canon AEl
Lens	24mm
Film	Ilford HP5

207

Photographer	Alec Ponton, UK
Location	Green Party Conference
Camera	Canon AEL
Lens	70–210mm Zoom
Film	Ilford Pan F

208

Photographer	Peter Elgar, UK
Location	After the party – Henley Regatta
Camera	Canon FT
Lens	100mm
Film	Ilford XP1

209

Photographer	Casimir Pudzianowski, West Germany
Location	Schwetzinger Zoo, West Germany
Camera	Nikon F3
Lens	35–200mm Zoom
Film	Kodachrome

210

Photographer	Adrienne Rogers, UK
Location	
Camera	Nikon FE2
Lens	75–150mm Zoom
Film	Kodachrome 64

211

Photographer	Paul Alexander, UK
Location	
Camera	Olympus OM1
Lens	50mm Soft Focus
Film	Scotch 1000

212

Photographer	Lo Nyian Loon, Sarawack
Location	Hawker at Sunday Market, Saba
Camera	Nikon FM
Lens	105mm
Film	

213

Photographer	Lucinda Beatty, UK
Location	Fresh Beancurd Hawker Yangshuo, Guangxi, China
Camera	Nikon FE
Lens	35mm
Film	EPD

214 Upper

Photographer	David Abiaw, UK
Location	Tower Bridge, London
Camera	Olympus OM1
Lens	50mm
Film	Kodak Ektachrome

214 Lower

Photographer	Alan Bell, UK
Location	
Camera	Nikon FE
Lens	200mm
Film	Kodak Ektachrome

215 Upper

Photographer	Steve Eaton, UK
Location	Humber Bridge at Twilight
Camera	Practika PM3
Lens	50mm
Film	Orwo 100

	215 Lower		221
Photographer	Keith Brown, UK	Photographer	Bizzie Frost, UK
Location	Cleveleys, Near Blackpool	Location	Peasant Farmer from Abha, Saudi Arabia
Camera	Minolta XGM	Camera	Pentax ME
Lens	50mm	Lens	35–135mm Zoom
Film	Ektachrome 100	Film	Kodachrome 64

	216–217		222–223
Photographer	David Johnston, UK	Photographer	Shivji, India
Location	Romany, Near Broadway, Worcester	Location	Desert in Rajasthan, India
Camera	Leica R4S	Camera	Pentax MX
Lens	90mm	Lens	135mm
Film	Kodak	Film	Kodak 25

	218–219		224
Photographer	Patrick Duzer, France	Photographer	Peter Wilkinson, UK
Location	Citroen CVs	Location	East Coast Estuary
Camera		Camera	From Disc-Size Negative
Lens		Lens	25mm
Film		Film	Agfa 1600

	220		Rear Endpaper
Photographer	David Johnston, UK	Photographer	Peter Rees, UK
Location	Ibizenco Peasant	Location	Princes Street, Edinburgh, Scotland
Camera	Leica R4S	Camera	Olympus OM1N
Lens	90mm	Lens	28mm
Film	Kodak	Film	Kodak HS Infra Red

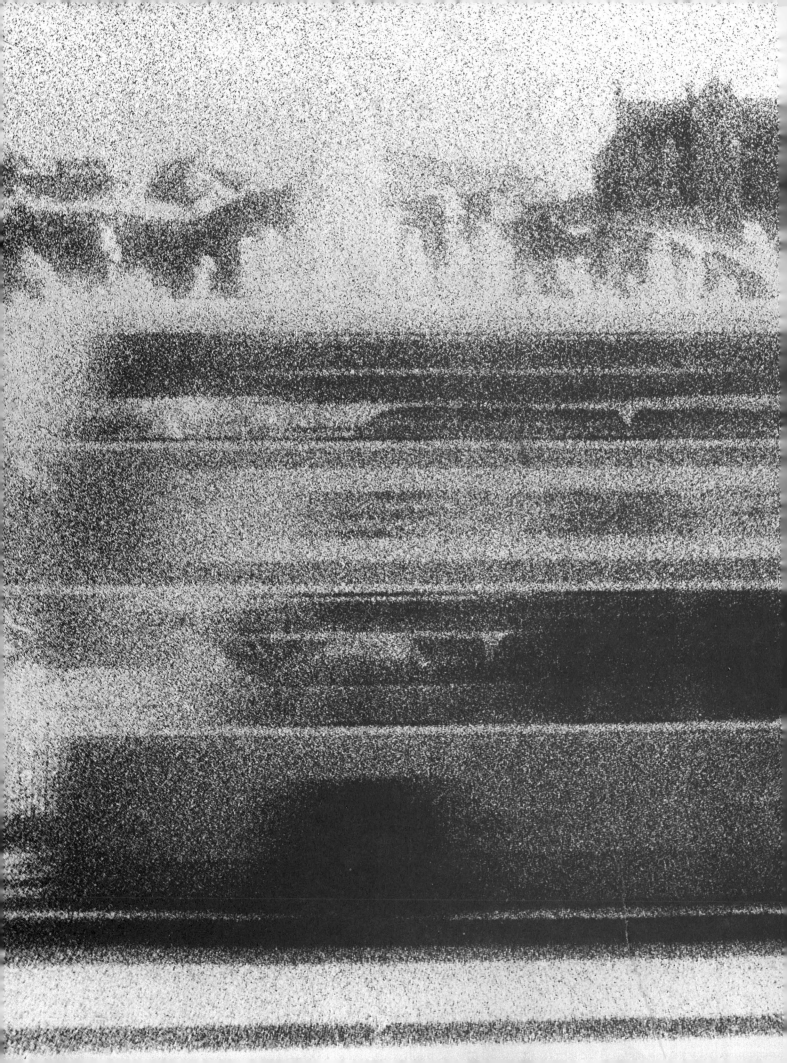